FEAR NOT

Roxy Fredrickson

ISBN:0989473562
ISBN-13:9780989473569

DEDICATION

This Book is dedicated to
God—my Father, who has
given me all that is necessary
for life and happiness and to
Don, my husband, who has
been a loving partner
through thick and thin
always being there for over
43 years.

CONTENTS

FOREWORD

I've thought and thought about how to begin this book and this is what has come to me today:

Something I have observed over the decades of my life is that there is a difference between children raised like I was versus children raised in homes where the father is of strong moral character and is a hands-on participator in rearing the children.

Children raised in this manner are virtually fearless! Yes, fearless! They are outspoken, brave individuals who go forth and conquer the world.

While this being a mere observation I wanted to take my observations a step further and apply them to our heavenly Father. He commands us—365 times to Fear NOT. That's one Fear NOT for every day of the year and when Father says it we should know that He has a plan and a purpose to bring this to fruition in our lives!

In the chapters following, I hope to open hearts and minds to allow God the Father, by the gift of His Son and the Holy Spirit, to be hands-on in our lives!

First off, if you have not received Jesus Christ as your personal Savior STOP right here! This is a must before you go any further. For all have fallen short of the Glory of God and have need of a Savior, this being Jesus Christ, Himself. Pray these words:

Jesus I am a sinner I need You to come into my heart and life. Please forgive me of all my sins. Accept me Lord into Your Kingdom as Your child by Your Grace and Mercy in

Christ Jesus'. Amen.

Yes, it's that simple to become a child of God as God the Father provided a way before we were even conceived. His plan and purpose always included us as His children and for Him to be a hands-on Father.

"Happy is the child who has God as his Father!"

CHAPTER 1
THE BEGINNING

Thirty years ago I walked into an appointment at the drug counselors' office and said to him, "I need help."

He said, "What's going on."

I told him that I had stopped drinking on my own but was white knuckling it right now and asked him, "Do I have to get in trouble with the law before I can get help?"

He said, "No," and immediately made a few phone calls to area treatment centers. They were full. "But," he said, "they can get you in for inpatient treatment in a few days."

"I can't go to inpatient treatment I have two kids ages 6 and 2!"

His immediate response was, "What kind of

mother are you now?" He saw I was back paddling and knew that if things didn't get settled right then and there I would not follow through with what I had been asking for.

I agreed that I wasn't much use as a mother with the way things were in my life, so I had to make some changes and that would begin by going for a 28 day treatment!

Amazing Grace how sweet the sound was the song I sang over and over to myself the night before I went into treatment. I knew I had failed as a human being and had not only let my family down I had let myself down. All the while, knowing that God had created me for something more than being a drunk and wasting my life.

As I walked up the steps to go into treatment my legs gave out I staggered as I went to the door. Thank God, there were people there who had been down this road and welcomed me with open arms. They ushered me into the reception room where someone quickly took me into another room and began my intake. Little did I know that in the next 28 days I would begin to know peace and contentment for the first time in my life.

Fear and rage had been the rulers in my head. Thank God I had been given a curious spirit as I had seen people having a goodtime without drinking and I wanted just that. God was always in my life chipping away at my resolve.

Sitting at the tables in AA I began to see something I really enjoyed and wanted from one person in particular who said she gave all the Glory to Jesus Christ, her higher power. I knew this gal was not just mouthing but had a walk that I admired and wanted. She invited the group of us over for coffee to her house and the adventure began.

There were a few years that passed before I got up enough courage to pray with her, but I remember it so vividly. As we knelt in her bedroom she began praying and laughing I slide half-way across the room. I never had heard anyone laugh while they were praying! It scared me—a lot! Time rolled on and my curious spirit would start asking questions.

I was teaching Sunday school at a Methodist church and learning right along with the kids The day of Pentecost had arrived and in my teacher's booklet it explained a bit about Pentecost but I wasn't to teach the kids about the baptism in the Holy Spirit with evidence of speaking in tongues as that wasn't for today.

Funny side bar—when I got to my class I asked them if they had ever heard about speaking in tongues. This one little girl said, "Yeah. It's like saying, 'Sold American.'" She spoke it like an auctioneer. I laughed and thanked her.

When I got home from church that day I called my friend and asked her if she had ever heard about speaking in tongues. The phone grew eerily silent for a few seconds. She said later that she had to contemplate telling me the truth about herself. Anyway, she said, "Roxy, I speak in tongues."

I dropped the phone—the hair on the back of my neck stood straight out. I knew that I knew there was something to this Jesus thing besides words. I knew that Jesus was real! Talk about seek and you will find! I had gone to church a lot in my younger years and had returned when I sobered up, cause I knew it was the right thing to do. But, never could I have fathomed what the Lord had in store for me.

In the following chapters I will, by the Grace of God, give you my account of the Holy Spirit working in my life. Lest anyone think I am someone special—I am and so are you. Let me remind you that God is no respecter of persons and that He loves all His children, for the price that was paid for them was the spilling of the blood of His precious Son.

The Word tells us that we are a peculiar people—that being a people bought with the priceless gift of the blood of Christ that we could become heirs of salvation. Do not be one of those that cry, "Lord, Lord," and do not the things that He says.

Be baptized in the Holy Spirit that you may have the Comforter, Counselor at your side to lead the way!

CHAPTER 2
OUR RESPONSE

Lamentations 3:57: *Thou* drew *near in the day that I called upon thee: Thou said FEAR NOT!*

Luke 12:32: *Fear not little flock, for it is your Father's good pleasure to give you the Kingdom.*

What would be your response if after calling out to the Lord He walked into the room and said to you, "Fear not?" This would all depend on how you saw your earthly father. Would your heart be filled with anguish and fear?

What type of a man is/was your father—austere? Absent? Overbearing? Non-committal i.e., wimpy? There in flesh but not in spirit? Drunkard? Workaholic? Good provider for material things but not really there for much else? In answering these questions we can get answers to other questions about how we see our heavenly Father.

Now that we understand that our perception of our Heavenly Father is akin to our earthly father, we can understand and see that our perceptions are askew and have need of repair. As I have stated earlier, God commands us to Fear Not and it all depends on how we look at these commands—with what type of eyes. He would be austere and foreboding in one person's eyes and wishy-washy in another's eyes.

Yes, I see you're getting the picture. Both being skewed perceptions of God the Father's intent. So when our Lord says that He, "will never leave us nor forsake us," the perception, once again, is askew. We think He says it but we aren't to take it to heart or, He says it and we are fearful that He will do something we hate, like make us into something we're not nor ever want to be. Well, well, well, kinda stuck are we! We need to stop wavering between two opinions. We ask for help but want it our way.

We are told and told again to believe but there are layers and layers of learned FEAR!

We must begin by acknowledging that there is fear and that if we are to get rid of it, we must let go and allow the Lord—by His Spirit—to remove the forbidden fruit. I say forbidden fruit, because we as God's children have no good reason to partner with fear. Fear can grab a hold of us all day long, but we do NOT have to take hold of it.

I believe this is what Father is telling us as He

says, "FEAR NOT." This, not to give us an unattainable task, but to give us choice! We have a Father who will allow us to go to hell if we so choose (not His will) but He never—I mean never—takes away our choices!

You ask, "What about all the bad things that have come my way? I didn't ask for them, I didn't choose them."

I will answer a question with a question. What did you do with them? Did you learn from them or did you allow them to make you bitter and fearful of the next time something bad would happen?

Case-in-point, most of us have 20/20 hindsight and we will learn from our journeys. That is, if we are willing to take a good look and be honest with ourselves about where we have taken a wrong turn or have seen a need met inappropriately. Rather than turning to our Father who is the source of all that is good in our lives, for direction, for supply, for encouragement, and most of all the love we need to sustain us, we most often look to man—other people.

One of the reasons I am writing this book is that, once read, we can no longer claim ignorance for our mistakes, miss turns, or foibles. Proverbs 3:5-6: *Trust in the Lord with all your heart – lean NOT on your own understanding – acknowledging Him in all our ways and HE will direct our path*. This is a picture of looking to God, the Abba (Daddy) Father, and repenting when we make a mistake, miss turn or foible. He's right there to help us on this journey. This is what I call Hands-On Fathering. We must allow Him to be the Father to us that was and is intended.

I've asked myself what is one of the biggest fears that one can face? Is it not of being alone? As I thought of this the Lord put on my heart—His utter loneliness before He created man. "Let us create man in our own image." Then He made woman from the man so that Adam would not be alone. God's plan from the very beginning was for us not to be alone and for Him to be a hands-on Father.

I pray that we allow Him to be the Father He set out to be.

Through the Lord's mercies we are not consumed, because He is a compassionate God and His mercies are new every day. He is a faithful God who is firm, stable, and permanent. God never changes. He is our portion; He loves us with a covenant, steadfast love. Therefore, we can put our hope in Him!

CHAPTER 3
THE FATHER'S LOVE

Hebrews 12:5-11 (paraphrased) Speaks of the disciplining of the Father to His children. If we do not receive His discipline we are not His but Illegitimate and that no discipline is joyful at the time, but is painful. Nevertheless, it is fruitful for those who have been trained by it.

One of my sincerest fears as I came to the Lord was that of His disciplining me because I had grown up in a home where discipline was hit and miss. Most of the time hit, otherwise, I was pretty much ignored and left to do my own thing.

Yikes, what a rude awakening this was as an adult! I had no boundaries and no discipline. Fear of everything was my mainstay. Even though I knew the Lord, I really didn't trust Him to see me through to fruitfulness. I knew what His Word said, but with my skewed perception of a father it was difficult at best to trust and to let go and let God....... I didn't know how to trust.

Father God showed me that the grapes did not get to be wine without crushing; nor did the wheat get to be bread without grinding; nor did the clay get to be a pot without first cutting the air out of the lump with a very sharp instrument. Then smacking it down on the table several times. Next, it was molded with water. All this, just to get ready for the furnace!

Now you say, "My—my! What's next?"

By His Grace, Father's Love has taught me over and over again that He only allowed discipline in my life for my profit that I might be a partaker of His kingdom. Just as was stated in the previous chapter, we are to Fear Not as it is His desire to give us the kingdom.

Longing for His kingdom, my journey would continue.

I had read in His Word about the Israelites wondering in the desert for 40 years—a nine day journey took them 40 years! Then to top it off their first leader, Moses, missed entering the promise land because of his disobedience. Although Moses had been used greatly by God, he still missed it. I am wondering why. Was it lack of discipline on His part?

In speaking to Christians I find that many are trapped in the fear of discipline, especially when their history has been similar to mine. Their fear of discipline is far stronger than their curiosity of what the kingdom of God is really like.

The Word tells us that righteousness, peace, and joy in the Holy Spirit are the Kingdom of God. These attributes being fruits we all would like to have. After discipline our Father says the outcome is a peaceful fruit of righteousness—wow! If we can only get past the fear of discipline, I see we can have His Kingdom right here and right now.

All of us have run into undisciplined children and we attribute this to bad parenting or lack of parenting. Well, if you were not parented very well and you are an adult, this is now your cross to bear unless you decide to turn it over to God and truly become His child, by allowing Him to disciple you.

It is no strange fact that to be a disciple takes discipline. Otherwise—I believe—we are counting ourselves out before we even start. No one wants to be around an undisciplined, spoiled brat, not even ourselves. *If we choose not to be disciplined we will indeed be orphans.*

We Have A Choice!

We can stay trapped by fear or be set free by discipline. Both hurt but one is for great profit on our part, the other is just continued injury. I know we are accustomed to injury and it being familiar seems the safest. Trust God and listen to what the Spirit is speaking to your heart right now—let go of the fear and take hold of what God has for you through His loving discipline.

Pray this prayer:

Dear Father God—Allow me by Your grace to receive Your discipline that I may reap from it all that You have for me—righteousness, peace, and joy in the Holy Spirit. Thank You Lord for treating me as Your child in the name of Jesus Christ. Amen.

CHAPTER 4
FATHER'S SECRET PLACE

As a child of God who has allowed discipline to come into my life I have been given certain privileges that bring me great joy. There is more to being a child of God than escaping hell. It is grand being a child of privilege and given access to the Father's Secret Place (my application).

> *Habakkuk 2:2-3: Then the Lord answered me and said: Write the vision and make it plain on tablets, that he may run who reads it. For the vision is yet for an appointed time; But at the end it will speak and it will not lie. Though it tarries, wait for it; Because it will surely come, It will not tarry.*

This had to be around 25 years ago. While my prayer partner and I were praying in my basement we were both taken to different places or into different visions. She saw Jesus as a lowly child in a manger being the joy and peace of the world. I saw Christ as our soon coming King. He had on a long, flowing, white robe with a purple sash with gold trim. His face was so bright! His eyes were as flames of fire. His beard and His hair were white as wool. He didn't speak but I knew He was our soon coming King.

Then a few years later I had another vision. As a child, I had a habit of going out of town a bit to some huge rocks. I loved to climb them and sun myself. These were huge slate slabs that had crevasses and small pockets of water that I would play in. In my vision I was looking into these pools of water. They were stagnant and virtually worthless for anything else but flies and mosquitoes.

As I watched this water, suddenly the rock aroused itself and became a mammoth. I then was no longer watching but a part of the mammoth moving very slowly at first, but then picking up speed. I saw it's tail wipe out those that sat in church pews that had not decided to be a part of the body of Christ that was now on the move. As the mammoth began to go faster and faster I saw the gates of hell breaking off their hinges—they just sprung off. The Mammoth represented the part of the church that HAS decided to become the Body of Christ. I believe that with such a church the gates of hell cannot prevail.

Sometime later I was given, what I call an open vision. This being of a golden oil that flowed out from under a door in heaven down the steps. I asked the

Lord to expand the vision. He showed me a river lined with trees so lush and beautiful. The river flowed into a huge reservoir, as if reserved for a later time. I believe I've seen drops from the reservoir overflow here to earth.

I also saw a dam and prayed the Lord would break the dam to allow the flow to come to earth But just as the dam broke I saw the very finger of God close the breach and with it came the knowledge that the flow was for an appointed time. I believe that time approaches as God's children come into alignment with His plan for them and His Kingdom.

I share all of this with you to give some insight into how God treats His children. He is a hands-on Father who has no favorites and would certainly share His Secret Place with all who would become His children.

CHAPTER 5
I WAS THERE!

As I grew in the Lord I began to see His sovereignty, omnipotence, omniscience, and His omnipresence. I came to a place in my walk that made me wonder where the Lord had been in my life during a tumultuous childhood. This all ended up with me shaking my fist at the Almighty God and asking Him where He was when I needed Him the most.

His reply—"I was there and I saw it all."

With this reply came the revelation of free-will. This became the beginning of my realizing that we live in a fallen world and that though our God is sovereign He has given us free will to take Him or leave Him to follow His precepts or not. The people in my life who had abused me had been given free will. Once again choice entered into the picture.

You see, I didn't realize I had choices until I

sobered up in treatment. The household that I grew up in was not big on choices—you just took what you were given and were supposed to be grateful no matter how you felt. So, my not understanding choice was part of the problem. "My people parish for lack of knowledge," say's the Lord. Boy! Did I lack knowledge in so many areas.

Sitting in church the next Sunday my conscience let me know that the Lord had seen everything I had done wrong as well. I thanked my Lord for forgiving my sin and washing it all away. Now—realizing that forgiveness is a two-way street—Dear Lord, forgive them for they knew not what they did. I thank the Lord for His forgiveness and His faithfulness.

On goes the journey—the Lord took me places in my past as He had been there and seen it all. He took me all the way back to the womb. I was in my mother's womb and my father and mother were arguing. I couldn't understand their words, but the part I could understand was their emotions.

My father's was rejection. My mother's was fear.

The Lord spoke to my heart and said, "Your earthly father might not have wanted you to be born, but that doesn't matter because I wanted you born!"

Wow! What washed over me at that moment was relief. I'd always felt unwanted as my father had left shortly after I was born. But, little did I know at the time my Heavenly Father was on the scene ready and waiting for me to acknowledge Him.

Another time the Lord took me back to my childhood I was running around the yard in my bare feet and had stepped in some dog dirt on the sidewalk. It was a hot summer day and the dirt was exceptionally mushy. There was a man laughing at me—not just laughing, but roaring. All I could do was cry. He hurt my feelings when he laughed at me and it made me angry and sad at the same time.

I couldn't figure out why the Lord would show me this until minutes later this man and I were in the back yard by the hose. The hose had lain in the sun and the water coming through it was warm and comforting on my foot as this man helped me wash my feet. I hadn't remembered the man helping me wash until just then.

This to me was such a picture of what the Lord had been sharing with me all along about forgiveness and the washing away of my sins. Also, that His only concern was that I be clean and happy.

CHAPTER 6
LOVE MY SON

The days in summer can be so full and plentiful that sometimes we forget that everything we do concerns our God. My journey continues as I keep reading in the Bible that I must love others as I love myself. For some reason, at first, this did not compute. Finally, one day out of pure frustration I asked the Lord how can I love myself without getting fat headed?

I went about my day tending to the kids and the household chores. I was walking up the back deck as I had been out to the clothesline hanging clothes when all of a sudden the Lord spoke to me audibly. He said "Love my Son because you and He are one in the same!"

Wow! Again, I had learned in treatment that I could no longer be the center of my universe, that my life would be much happier being centered around a higher power. Now here my God was telling me to love Jesus and I would automatically love myself correctly. This made perfect sense but, didn't feel I could share this as it sounded like I thought I was Christ.

It took me quite a while to figure out that this meant that I was His child just like Jesus was His Son, and keeping my eyes on Jesus was going to lead me into everything that God had for me! Not only was I going to love, but I could allow myself to be loved!

I can remember the first time I heard my husband tell me he loved me—I said the first time I heard it— not that he hadn't said it before. My head fell between my knees and I cried like a baby or should I say I howled. That's what they must mean when they say love hurts—it literally hurt me 'cause it went so deep.

The love tore through so many layers of anguish and pain that I could only cry and say, "Thank You, Lord."

My poor husband probably thought I was nuts as he was good to me and he'd always told me he loved me. My husband was the first man in my life that didn't leave me when the going got rough. Now, that's love!

Just to give a little background. As I said earlier, my father left shortly after I was born and then my mother and my step-father divorced when I was ten. My step-father was the kind of man that wanted things his way and that was that—no choice there. He wanted me a certain way, wanted me to eat what he wanted me to, and wanted me to sleep the way he wanted me to. (Walking through all of this with the Lord was miraculous.)

When it was bedtime we weren't allowed to talk and giggle. We just had to go to bed and go to sleep. Well, if anyone knows kids, that's all you have to do to get kids giggling is let them know they can't giggle.

Sis and I would try our hardest not to giggle but just couldn't help ourselves. When one would start the other would chime in. Well, before long our step-father would get wind of our giggle and come into the bedroom with a strap that he had made just for the occasion and he would whip us—into silence.

As the Lord brought me back to this very incident, He was with me and I knew it this time. I stood in the bed and looked straight at my step-father and said. "E..... in the Name of Jesus Christ I forgive you...."

With that his head dropped—his arm dropped to his side—and he turned and left the room. It's as if the event never happened. God be praised as His forgiveness flowed through me more healing and more peace abounded.

MY SEEKING CONTINUES

In the years to follow I had several encounters with the Lord. I finally asked my friend if she felt it was OK for me to ask the Lord if I could have the baptism of the Holy Spirit. (I thought you had to be someone special or, "holier than thou.") She said of course, we will ask him together. We prayed and asked, but

nothing happened. I sought and sought but nothing—
even to the point of going underwater with my mouth
open! Don't really know how I expected Him to help
me there—I came up from under the water sputtering,
but no tongues!

My seeking had gone on for six months when I
heard the Lord very clearly say to me three times,
"Get thee Baptized." I had been sprinkled as a kid
when I was confirmed in the Lutheran faith, but felt
that the Lord meant business. So, if I meant business
I'd better do what He told me to do.

My friend and I went to a Pentecostal church on
New Year's Eve that year and I so enjoyed the praise
and worship and the fellowship that followed. I made
an appointment with the pastor to talk to him about
getting baptized. The following Sunday I was baptized
but still no tongues.

In the following week I continued seeking the Lord
and not long after, I was kneeling in my bedroom
when my tongue began moving—as if on its own—
powerful—a power I had never experienced before! I
was now baptized in the Holy Spirit with the evidence
of speaking in tongues.

I whispered when I prayed for the first two week as
the power was so big it frightened me. This is when I
first realized that the Lord's command to FEAR NOT
had teeth. I truly had been given a Spirit of Power,
Love and Sound Mind!

I have just realized as of this writing that the reason
why the Spirit was sooooo strong was because of all
the Word of God that was stored up in my spirit by

memorizing when I was a child and studying to be confirmed in the Lutheran church.

This is another example of FEAR NOT because our Lord will work all things together for GOOD!

CHAPTER 7
PASSION LOST TO PASSION FOUND

The Holy Spirit took me back to where I lost my passion. This was through a deep hurt. This hurt positioned me to do my will not the Lord's. I've learned through experience in the Holy Spirit that as a child and as an adult child that I experience pain by encapsulating it and putting it into compartments.

Oh yes, I acknowledge the pain. But I'm realizing that I also have allowed the pain to put in me a fear of going down the same road as whatever the experience that had hurt me. I always must realize that I experience that pain through who I was then and, also, who I am now.

Example: I believe the Holy Spirit has revealed to me that I lost my passion after having poured out my life for a church and then our pastor left, leaving me feeling abandoned. I felt that I had lost my outlet for what the Lord had put into me and have been afraid to connect with anything that would be an outlet for that which the Lord puts in me. Kinda like shooting myself in the foot.

My life has lacked passion and the desire I once had for being about my Father's business. This had become buried under pain and fear. The fear disguising itself in self-will and stubbornness. Self-will in the fact that I felt like a chump when my church life fell apart and stubbornness feeling that I would never allow that to happen to me again!

The Holy Spirit revealed to me just this evening that this is what has happened and He will be taking me to the place we left off and picking up the pieces to resume our ministry! The fear that I have been experiencing about connecting with a body of believers will have to be overcome and will be overcome by the power of the Holy Spirit. "Not by power nor by might but by My Spirit,"—says the LORD! He that is in me is greater than he that is in the world.

No more will I allow this fear to control me nor will I let the enemy win. How great is thy faithfulness LORD unto me.

Serving was my passion and joy. I had forgotten that serving the Lord is the most thrilling thing on earth. Much pain could be avoided if I left it up to Him as to who it was I was to serve and not be serving who I felt I wanted to serve (the passion robber)—or who I felt was deserving to serve—or who I wanted to get close to (talk about self-serving and manipulative)....... No wonder I felt manipulated and not loved.

The Story:

Here I was put in a town that I disliked, surrounded by people I couldn't connect with— sounds like one of those impossible positions that our Lord is famous for allowing us to overcome! Try as I might I couldn't seem to connect with the little town or its people. The people seemed idealistically opposed to me or any position I took.

Having been blessed with 30 years of sobriety I felt I knew a thing or two, but was quick to find out that I didn't know much if anything! Every time I heard the word LOVE I cringed and felt backed into a corner by a controlling force that was strong-arming me. If I wasn't going do to things in love they wouldn't be accepted at all.

<u>Stuck</u> was the position I was in
and frustrated was an understatement.

Knowing all along that the Lord could and would get me to a place of forgiveness, healing, and passion—once again I relied on Him to do it all as I couldn't. He could and I just needed to allow Him by the Holy Spirit to "fix me!"

"Trust and obey for there is no other way to be happy in Jesus than to Trust and obey."

Not my will, but thine be done! I believe anything short of that allows me to be robbed of passion and joy!

Realizing it didn't matter where I was or who I was with but that as long as I was about the Father's business—His being a business of serving—my passion would be intact.

Now, I am speaking about myself and if this applies to you, please allow the Holy Spirit to lead you in the way of your service. It will be one of the most passionate, fulfilling times of your life!

CHAPTER 8
REJECTION, PRIDE, AND GRACE

FEAR NOT WHAT MAN CAN DO TO YOU – FOR HAVE I NOT SAID I WILL NEVER LEAVE YOU NOR FORSAKE YOU – SAYS THE LORD.
HEBREWS 13:5

The pain of rejection is fierce and deadly, it kills dreams and if it could it would kill us. This pain may cause one to walk away from their dreams and hopes. Know that this is exactly what the enemy would have us do.

Yes, it hurts, but as someone said, "Find a purpose for your pain." This will give you exactly what you need to pursue what the Lord has for you. Many people can see that you are talented and they are threatened by this; your talents for some reason make them feel inadequate. Their reaction to the feeling of threat is one of rejection.

Jesus said that He would never leave us nor forsake us. He bore our sins on the cross that we wouldn't have to be rejected. This goes for us, but also for those that are feeling threatened by our giftings.

My prayer would be that we could all come to the knowledge of that price that was paid for our freedom—freedom to be who God has created us to be. Not square pegs in round holes, just filling positions and jobs that need filling with the idea that, "If we don't do it, it won't get done!"

Just maybe some thing's shouldn't be done—right at this time—but can wait for the timing of the Lord—be done in His time and fashion—to accomplish His Will—His Way—and for His Purpose.

Taking a step back can help us to realize once again that we are not human doings but human beings who have been given the opportunity to be sons and daughters of the Most High God. Let Him be in control. Not my will but Thine Be Done!

Pride is an enmity to God. It is a sin that blinds man to his own thoughtlessness and rebellion against the very God he believes he is serving. Are you a fool to pride? Ask yourself, "Am I being a fool for the devil? Am I being used for the purpose of making my brother stumble. Or, is Grace abounding in my life? Am I encouraging my brother and looking out for his welfare?"

It really is quite easy to see where we are if we

just take a look. If we find ourselves in pride—we must Repent—and let Grace abound to us so all who surround us will see His victory in us! Our Savior, Jesus Christ, came to set the captives free. By allowing ourselves to see and repent of our wrongdoings it gives Grace to the body and wellness to all its bones…….

Something the body needs badly!

CHAPTER 9
THE SOLVING OF A RIDDLE

Why did I get sick and what was the plan? I know what God had promised me and I also know His Word that says He "will never leave me nor forsake me."

In the days and weeks leading up to my healing, God was busy at work peeling back the layers of misconception and darkness. Little did I know what He had in store for me, but as always I, like you, have 20/20 hindsight.

In my hindsight, I saw myself being prayed over for a new level of the prophetic, dreams and insight by the Holy Spirit. The dreams began right away, but what was the highlight for me was the anger my mom had towards me and pretty much everything.

Growing up I had never seen my mom as being an angry woman. After her death I saw her more as a saint having raised us kids all by herself. In fact, it took me a few days just to recognize that this is what the Holy Spirit was showing me and that I had taken this very personal. I believe children of angry parents take on a persona of the victim and are stuck there until we realize that the Lord has set us free.

My first misconception was that I hadn't seen my mother as being angry—just fearful. Previously the Lord had shown me that I vacillated between fear and anger 'cause anger made me feel strong. My reasoning was, "Where did I get this behavior from?" Light bulb time! I was taught this by the environment I had grown up in.

Yikes! Simplicity can be complicated!

I had always blamed my birth father for all our problems. He had abandoned us when I was 10 months old. It was not until one day I was in the doctor's office and the attendant was asking me about my history—illnesses in the family—and I couldn't believe what came out of my mouth when she asked me about my father. I said, "That bastard left when I was 10 months old and I don't know anything about him." This statement really bothered me as I thought I had forgiven him and the situation years prior to this.

Out of the fullness of the heart the mouth speaks!

I went to our leader at church and told him what had happened and He said, "You're cursing a dead man." My reasoning was that he had left and our lives had been set on a course of poverty that was not retrievable and that my life was forever scarred by this abandonment. I had just taken on the persona of my mom.

She always blamed him for everything negative that happened in our lives, not doing the adult thing and reassuring us that things would be okay. Not telling us that life does give us some lemons sometimes. We have our choice—make lemonade or suck on sour lemons the rest of our lives.

"My people parish for lack of Knowledge."

Wow did this apply! I could, no longer blame my father for my negativity so I must forgive and let go of the negative. This allowed me to see my mother's issues more clearly as well as my own.

I had dealt with anger and fear and the Lord had restored my JOY! I thought I had dealt with everything in this area that was possible or that I had to deal with. This was another round of struggle that had to be dealt with by a letting go and letting God so to speak.

Upon realizing this I have struggled until I could struggle no more and have finally seen what it is the Lord would have me see. He had allowed the pain to come forth so that I could give it to Abba allowing Him, by the Spirit, to wash and cleanse these old wounds of mine allowing healing to proceed as planned by my Lord and Savior, Jesus Christ...... By whose strips I've been healed!

Forgiving my mom for not having the knowledge or seeking the Lord for what she needed has solved the riddle of my own life.

CHAPTER 10
YIELDED AND STILL

In the days, weeks, and months ahead I spent most of my time in the Word of God and prayer. Rediscovering my life in Christ—reliving many situations in my life—but now, with the knowledge of Christ.

I was seeing each and every situation from His view point. I began allowing Him to take the gnarly roots of my past, dip them in the balm of Gilead and remove other things that were harming me. I saw Him remove shame from me and I also saw my flesh trying to grab it back. Shame was something I had learned to live with and had even seen it as humbleness as false humbleness. That is what the Lord informed me was not humbleness at all, but a false <u>pride</u>.

Shame is the enemy's tool to keep you under his thumb, just as if a sibling of yours saw you do something wrong and reminded you of it every chance they got!

As I lay there asking God to remove anything that wasn't of Him I saw an eel like being—big and black—leaving my body, but what shocked me was the gnarly hand that tried to grab it back. The one leaving was shame and the one trying to grab it back was my flesh.

Days later as I was doing house chores, I felt this ominous darkness trying to come over me. I had been studying spiritual warfare and knew of the armor of God I knew I had to do something offensive to rid myself of this darkness trying to come on me. I picked up the sword of the Spirit as I saw this eel like presence trying to come on me again. I slit it up the middle and cut it in pieces and flicked its pieces into the pit of hell! Victory once again as this had been shame trying to come back on me.

He whom the Son sets free is free indeed!

Let me tell you about shame. I look at this as if I had a masquerading enemy—one that seemed like humility but was false pride that kept me in prison. Every time I started to do something for the Lord I had this overwhelming sense of pride and I knew that was wrong. Then I would start picking on myself—"You're not good enough"—and the such. Until one day the Lord pointed out to me that this was false pride and that to receive the abundant life that He had provided I would need to allow Him to remove this from me. Little did I know at the time that it's name was shame.

I felt shame and didn't know why. Yes, I had done things that I wasn't proud of and had had things done to me that...hurt. But this was not about me any longer. This was about Jesus and why He went to the cross. It was for my peace and sanctification and this shame was standing in the way—batting anything good away from me that the Lord offered through His sacrifice. That's when I laid there and said Lord, "Take anything away from me that is not of You," and He did!

The flesh will try to hold unto what is familiar so be cautious not to let the flesh win. Even though a newfound peace may feel strange—allow this peace to permeate your soul and you will know that all is well and that you have indeed allowed the Lord to be LORD in your life.

CHAPTER 11
EXPOSING SATAN

The Lord has said in His Word that I am to be angry and sin not. Well, I am angry at Satan—he stole my childhood. You know what they say about taking candy from a baby—that is exactly what he did. God had given me a yearning for Himself and a longing to belong to something or someone. Satan, knowing full well that I possessed this yearning, took advantage of me and my circumstances.

Being raised in a single-parent family isn't easy for anyone. Mom worked most of the time and we children were left to raise ourselves. I was seduced at a very early 6 to 8 years of age, into thinking I could have my needs met by doing what I knew was wrong, but it was, "our little secret."

I believe that the enemy loves secrecy and uses it always to his advantage. It made me feel safe and secure at the moment and cared for. Now that I look back. Life seemed safe and secure in our little secret until someone found out and it stopped with no explanation. I felt out in the cold and unloved and so ashamed. Along with the rejection came my stance that I wouldn't let anyone hurt me again. Therefore, the thieving ways of the enemy continued in my life.

From that day forward I never trusted anyone or anything to do right by me in my life. Walls of hatred and misunderstanding so thick it would take dynamite to get them down formed around me.

Yes indeed, the Lord was there and saw it all.
Praise His Holy Name.

He was there with the dynamite all the time, just looking to me for the okay to blast down the walls and invade my life with His Spirit. The Lord showed me by His Spirit that all the hate, anger, and shame that I held for everyone, mostly myself, were doorways in which the enemy could come and go as he pleased. In fact, he only had to come in every once in a while and stir things up, otherwise, I pretty much took care of messing things up myself.

What a mess my life had become and I only had myself to blame, but, of course, I blamed everyone else. It wasn't until I went into rehab all those years later that I learned to own what I had done and start repairing the damage or should I say—allowing the Lord to repair the damage. To this day the process is still continuing and I presume that it will continue until the day I die.

My purpose in all of this is to expose how satan takes advantage. But knowing the Lord today allows me to expose satan for what he is—a thief, a killer, and a destroyer. Don't doubt in your mind what he will do to your unsuspecting children! Protect them and teach them the Word of God and the power of the indwelling Holy Spirit so they can protect themselves from the one that goes prowling around seeking whom he may devour.

He doesn't care if they're seemingly helpless children or not. He knows the plans that God has for each and every one of us and he means to see those plans sidetracked or destroyed all together. That old song keeps going through me—"I went to the enemies camp and I took back what he stole from me, took back what he stole from me, took back what he stole from me…."

Hallelujah! Hallelujah! Hallelujah!

And I caught him in the act so he owes me seven times that which was stolen. There is no amount of money you can put on a childhood but from where I sit it's got to be worth millions and billions!

Questioning myself—Why do I feel that I still have areas in my life that are open to what I don't want them to be. Answering the Lord shows me that I continue to fill up the God given need in me by things other than Him!

Dear Lord,

By Your grace and through the shed blood of Christ, I ask that You fill in any and all areas that are created by You, Lord, that are to contain You.
Please fill them as only You can.
Let me, by Your grace, operate and give of You not out of my emptiness or wantonness. Let there be only room given for the things of God and not anything else of myself or the world.
I hunger for this as one that needs air to breath.
My weariness is that of one that has labored for a very long time, seeking peace and righteousness.
Help my mind to grasp those things that are given to me freely that I may live and breathe in them as one who walks in complete freedom—allowing my renewed mind to own freely all that the Lord has given,
remembering that I was created by God for His plan and purpose,
His way!
Furthermore, in the name of Jesus Christ I forgive myself of ignorance and stubbornness!
My Father shall supply all my need according to His riches in glory by Christ Jesus! He did not put in me a need that He didn't intend to meet! He did not allow a hole in me that He didn't intend to fill! Just as the earth was created to show us His glory so were we all created!

Let Your glory shine that all men will see it and be glorified in Christ Jesus!

Cracks are merely the places in me that I haven't allowed my Father to fill when exposed. Places that, if exposed, satan will use them against me. If given to the Lord, He will fill them and be glorified. If they remain cracks they give the enemy an in—if they are filled with the truth of God there will be a "No Admittance" sign on them.

Let's say the enemy sees a crack called fear. He will take it and run crying, "Poor me. I can do nothing by myself, I need so much I will never have enough." If the enemy is met by the truth he falls flat and can do nothing as he was defeated by the price our Lord and Savior Jesus Christ paid for us.

We being children of the Most High God have every right to answer any question with the Word of God! Our answer to fear can be, "We have not been given a spirit of fear, but we have been given a spirit of adoption whereby we cry ABBA, Father." Or, "We have not been given a spirit of fear but of power, love and a sound mind!" Take that you devil—one that will take advantage wherever he can—so be careful for he goes around seeking whom he may devour.

Find out what you are fearing and allow the Lord to fill that crack with His Word! Ask yourself when you fear, "What is it that I am fearing?" Then go to the Word and fill in the crack with that Word that applies so you will be ready to answer when the enemy calls.

CHAPTER 12
THE HEALING

When I was 12 years old I was diagnosed with Rheumatoid Arthritis and given a sentence of this for life. I was told to take aspirin until my ears rang for the pain and sent home. Through the years and with a plethora of medicines, my health has been maintained to be good, but I know that I know—the Lord has the best health in mind for me.

Today as I recalled, with the Father's help, a time just before I had been diagnosed when my sister and I had been left at the carnival. Our brother's had been assigned to pick us up but had failed to do just that. Sis and I were roaming around the carnival and it was getting late the carnival closed at midnight and the hour was approaching.

I can remember being very scared and Sis telling me to be quiet as I had a tendency to whimper when afraid. We approached a policeman to tell him of our dilemma and he immediately took control of the situation and got ahold of our mother. The next thing I remember is our mother picking us up and her being very angry. She was upset at our brother's and upset in general as she was embarrassed that this situation even happened.

I believe today that our mother was a very fearful and passive-aggressive woman. I've been given the understanding that in her day it wasn't lady like to be angry so she hid her anger pretty well, except for those times when she couldn't!

The next memory I have is of being home in bed and having a convulsion. I believe that something entered into my body that night from the tumult of being left and of my mother's anger at the situation that caused my system to register rheumatoid arthritis and I—by the strength and glory of God accept the healing of His touch in this area of my life.

I surrender all the pain and fear to God—all the anger and striving to my Abba Father—and accept His full healing in my soul and body. He has promised me heavenly bone and that nothing—but nothing—touches heavenly bone.

I praise and thank You, Lord, for the heavenly bones that You have given me that my immune system is restored to normal function that all the areas that were previously involved be healed, set free and giving glory to God!

I thank You Lord for loving me when I couldn't love myself and believing in me when I didn't have faith to move this mountain. By faith and by Your grace this mountain has been moved and will be cast into the sea where it will be remembered no more!

God be Praised!

The days and weeks ahead will be transformation time for me I can feel my body responding to Your Word, by faith, right now Lord! (At the time of this printing the full manifestation of this healing is yet to come, your continued prayers are requested.)

CHAPTER 13
TRADITIONS OF MAN
Making The Word Of God
Of No Effect

The Word of God is as a two edged sword—one of, if not the most, powerful thing we possess as children of God. To be spoken forth, the Word breaks down walls and brings into existence what the Father intends for His children. The power of the Word is to give the children of God all that is theirs by the knowledge and application.

- Application brings wisdom.
  - The Word = knowledge
    - Knowledge + application = Wisdom.

Free will, enters all facets of our lives. Father God, by His Grace and Wisdom, gave His children free will. He has even given us free will even to the point of allowing us to refuse Him. Again, we have choice to receive His Word and apply it. Unless we, as God's children, adopt His way of doing things there is only half an adoption here and we will remain in the dark!

If we by disobedience hear the Word of God and do not obey we have an orphan soul. Choosing to not receive disciplining from the Father leaves us in the position of illegitimacy. So basically we can be in word Christian, but not in soul and remain this way for years until we see it.

Dear Lord, Open our eyes to see
our disobedience.

The Lord has shown me that if indeed we through disobedience become illegitimate in our soul from His kingdom, this does not mean that we are just left to our own devices we are immediately scooped up by the kingdom of darkness and are open to all forms of rebellion and witchcraft. Sounds strong, I believe this to be true.

I see the spirit of Jezebel (controlling, defiant spirit) around God's church all the time. At first I became overwhelmed at the knowledge of this, but the Lord said to me, "Be of good courage for I have overcome the world!"

Dear Father, Open our eyes to the Orphan soul. Help
us through Your Spirit to walk free of the
imprisonment of the enemy. We acknowledge You in
this matter and by faith believe that You will direct our
path. In the name of Jesus Christ I pray.
Amen

God's callings and giftings are given without repentance—meaning that the call and giftings we have been given as children of God will still operate in a soulish rebellion. The first mark of this is when we take the gifts of God, apply them to any given situation and they bring glory to us not God the Father. I'm not speaking of people seeing you as great for your giftings. It's when the gifts of God are used for self-gratification to make yourself feel good about you.

Don't be fooled (examine the fruit). If you are still operating in the gifts of God and do not have His wonderful peace you need to examine yourself immediately.

Dear Father,
Examine my heart, show me by Your Spirit what is off and create in me a clean heart and renew a right spirit within me.
Thank You Lord that You, Jesus Christ, are the anchor of my soul and my compass.
In the name of Jesus Christ we praise and thank You Lord.
Amen!

CHAPTER 14
THE GUT, THE SOUL,
AND
THE SPIRIT!

The Gut the Soul and the Spirit!

The gut is unreliable, the soul is emotional, but the Spirit is undeniably here and ready to be recognized as the lover of all that is good and acceptable to the Lord!

For years I had relied on my gut to guide my choices and thinking. Realizing that my gut used the "If it feels good do it" route, helped me to realize the dangerous roads my gut had taken me on!

Then my soul came into play as, "How does this make you feel?" Once again I realized that feelings are not truth or fact—they just are there to enhance ones pleasure. They are not intended to be an indicator of direction one should take on this road of life.

Ah yes, my born again Spirit, jumping up and down with joy as I realize that all along this is the exact one I should listen to and heed if I am to have a fulfilling, fruitful life in the Lord!

Deep in my gut and soul lurked many dark areas that my spirit had gone to and lit up so that the Lord could heal them. In the previous chapters I have shared with you, the reader, about the rubble that had been in my soul and that rubble had buried my spirit and hid it from me.

It was only through the grace of God and the Holy Spirit that my own spirit has been uncovered and rediscovered. She is as a gleeful child ready to do the bidding of the Lord.

By the grace of God may I continue to have this dance with her!

ABOUT THE AUTHOR

Born in Minnesota, Roxy now lives in the Pacific Northwest with her husband and Buster, their four-legged, furry friend. She and her husband raised two children and have one and half grandchildren. Life experiences have enriched and evoked her to share her triumphs in the Lord through the writing of this book.

As you walk through her life, may you be emboldened to allow yourself to "Let go and let God!"